Things My Mother Never Taught Me

Kayla D. Miller

BookLeaf Publishing

India | USA | UK

Presentation by *BookLeaf Publishing*

Web: www.bookleafpub.com

E-mail: info@bookleafpub.com

ISBN: 9789358369298

First edition 2023

DEDICATION

In loving adoration and memory of the beautiful Etta Lenora.

This book is for you, Maw-Maw.

I feel you smiling down from Heaven on me daily and I hope that you are proud of the woman I have become.

ACKNOWLEDGEMENT

My first book! Can you believe it?!
I stand at the threshold of a new journey, a
collection of words and emotions that have
poured from the depths of my soul. I am truly
overwhelmed with gratitude. There will never be
enough words to adequately express my
appreciation for the unwavering love and
support that I have received throughout the years
that have led to this moment. But I will surely
try.

To Mom and Dad - My fondest childhood
memories all center around the stories we would
read each night before bed. Those pivotal
moments shaped my hunger for knowledge and
my constant need to have my nose stuck in a
book. My life was idyllic from the start. As
parents you made sure that growing up was as
easy as possible and always encouraged me to
follow my dreams in whatever form they took.

To Mel - I am honored to have a strong woman
like you in my life. I know we haven't always
agreed on everything, but one thing that has
always remained has been the immense respect

that I have for you. You inspire me to push myself even further.

To my Aunt Mary - I will never forget the day I made the official go-ahead to publish and I called you. The first words out of your mouth were "You're shittin' me!" Which is honestly an apt response because, at that point, I wasn't even sure if this would come to be – but here we are and I am still in shock. You have continued to be my cheerleader, encouraging me to grow and become the woman that I am. I will never be able to fully thank you for all that you do for me.

To Liz and Heather – the two of you are truly two of the best friends a girl could ask for. Thank you for making Charleston a home and not just a temporary stop. Having two strong women by my side each and every day is a blessing and I am so thankful for you.

And Finally - To Joe – you put up with SOOOO much from me, all the late nights, the outbursts from being hangry, the stress tears, or whatever other ways my emotions took form. You have enriched my life in so many ways and daily I am in awe of and inspired by you. Thank you for sticking by me as I embrace and fulfill my dreams.

PREFACE

In the quiet moments of reflection, when the weight of our thoughts becomes almost tangible, we often find ourselves searching for guidance, for answers that have eluded us. It is during these times that we turn to the voices of the past, seeking solace in the wisdom of those who came before us. But what happens when the answers we seek cannot be found in the teachings of our mothers?

This collection of poetry, aptly titled "Things My Mother Never Taught Me," is a testament to the power of self-discovery, resilience, and the untold stories that shape us. It delves into the intimate corners of our lives, exploring the unspoken truths, the lingering uncertainties, and the poignant moments that shape our existence. Within these pages, you will encounter a journey that (hopefully) resonates with the human experience. The verses contained herein are woven with threads of love, loss, longing, and redemption, a tapestry of lessons learned and pure emotions felt. They capture the essence of what it means to navigate the complexities of life, all the while grappling with learning the hard lessons that our mothers hoped they would never have to teach.

I began writing these poems as a form of therapy. A way to become aware of my emotions and move past debilitating grief and longing. These poems are all based on true events and follow my journey to self-discovery where I learned to find strength within myself, even when the world knocked me down. These poems are a testament to the indomitable spirit that resides within each of us, reminding us that we possess the power to rise above adversity, even in the absence of guidance. Within the pages of this book, I speak openly about grief, sorrow, sexual assault, redemption, and love in hopes that you, dear reader, can find solace and even joy through my experiences.

For so many years after my sexual assault, I felt powerless, this collection is an invitation in the exploration of uncharted territories in the many stages of trauma. While I am not saying I am glad that it happened, that day altered the course of my life, forced me to embrace the complexities of my existence, and learn to embrace the power of my own voice. "Things My Mother Never Taught Me" is a beautiful agglomeration of the lessons I learned, often the hard way. May these poems, colored with my deepest desires, fears, and thoughts evoke emotions that allow words and memories to dance through your consciousness like gentle waves lapping the sand, guiding you out into a deeper understanding of the world around you. May you always know that your trauma does not have to define you and that if cultivated properly, can blossom into something beautiful.

The decision to publish this work was not one that I approached lightly, and it is my sincerest hope that you are as touched by reading it as I was by writing it.

With heartfelt gratitude,
Kayla D. Miller

If you or someone you know has been a victim of sexual assault – please call 1-800-656-4673 to be routed to a local sexual assault service provider in your area.

Golden Hour Perseverance

In the golden hours of twilight's embrace,
Words take flight and dreams find space,
Weaving a tapestry of poetic grace.
Stars paint the canvas of the midnight sky,
Moonbeams whisper, waves ebb and flow with
the tides,
A symphony of sounds dance, emotions laid to
the side.

In nature's arms, there's solace and peace,
Rivers meander, worries release
Nature's orchestra celebrates
the secrets within life's masterpiece.

The rhythm guides me, in melodies I dwell,
Joyous sonnets cast wistful spells,
Sparking memories with each sound, with each
smell.
Nature doesn't care about triumphs or struggles
or stories untold.
In Mother Earth's sanctuary, hearts are
unconditionally consoled.

In nature's embrace, my soul takes flight,
These moments, an escape from the plight,
A tapestry woven of life's infinite light.

A constant reminder that beauty is always near,
A journey lived, a perpetual reason to persevere.

My Best Friend

A confidant true
Souls dancing in harmony
Words are not needed

A listening ear
Love unconditional
In you, I confide

Silent guardian
Curiously watching every move
Through contemplative eyes

Purrs that mend the heart
A playful nudge, lets me know
I am not alone

Beautiful creature
The purest friendship I've known
A pillar of strength

Little white cat
Fur so soft, paws so gentle,
Who rescued whom?

I pack my grief in a box

I packed my grief in a box.
I sealed it shut.
I threw away the key to the lock.
Only to open it when I need to feel you near.

I nestle myself in cherished memories.
The painted canvas of my existence.
Stories and laughter echoing in my mind
A culmination of all the little things that matter
most.
Indelible imprints left.
Oh, how I have missed you.
Oh, how I have wept.
You graced our world with love so true

But you had to go.
Leaving behind wisdom in whispers on the
breeze.
A legacy etched in a sacred scroll,
And though the pain often weighs heavy on my
soul,
I move forward.
Embracing the little moments.

I pack my grief in a box,

I seal it shut
I throw away the key to the lock.
Only to open it again when I need to feel you
near.

Young Hearts Afire

In youthful hearts, a tale is spun,
Love awakens like the morning sun.
With innocence and wonder, passion ignites.
First love's flame, shining pure and bright.
Young souls learning the power of a beating
heart,
Sets the stage for love's immortal art.
Stolen glances, possibilities untold.
Navigating young love's unpredictable hold.
Uncharted realms explored hand in hand,
Creating memories, like grains of sand.
Every moment, a song, sung sweet and tender
Every kiss sparks memories to always
remember.
The imprint of first love forever remains.
A cut etched in our souls runs warm in our
veins.
First love should be cherished, those feelings are
rare.
A tiny flame, the smallest spark, eternally there.

Dancing on Broken Glass

We found love, tainted and bound
by chains unwound
A tragic dance, a twisted symphony,
Pain masqueraded as sweet harmony

In the beginning a flame so bright,
But jealousy marred even the happiest of times
Words withheld until it was too late,
Dripped like venom, filled with hate.

A careful dance we twirled on fragile glass,
afraid to break.
Afraid to move on, avoiding the ache.
We couldn't let the other go, so we trudged on
under the guise of love
Awaiting some sign, some signal from above.

You've moved on and so have I,
Both leaving shattered hearts in our wake.
I reclaimed my light, and so did you.
We both found healing, in a love anew.

In letting go we found our release,
And embraced a truer love that brings us both
peace.

The Story she Never Told

"Stop"
"NO"
"Don't"
Does anyone out there hear me SCREAMing?!
"HELP!"
A firm hand closes around my throat. I am
choking.
How could I let this happen?

It ends. Run away.
Turn on the shower. Scalding Hot
Scrub and scrub until the pain and the shame
have washed down the drain
Cover the bruises. Paste on a smile.
It's working. No one notices.
How could I let this happen?

I drank too much.
How could I let this happen?

Aren't we friends?
How could I let this happen?

Why can't I speak?
How could I let this happen?

You took everything from me
How Could I let this happen?

You took my pride
How could I let this happen?

You took my dignity
How could I let this happen?

My life will never be the same.
Do you even remember my name?

How could I let this happen?

How could I let this happen?

How could I let this happen?

Years later, the power is still yours
Acceptance is a daily battle.
But one thing has changed
There is no longer self-hatred
Only you are to blame.
HOW COULD YOU LET THIS HAPPEN?

The Lucky One

I was the lucky one.
Even though you left a hole in my soul and took
away things I will never get back.
I was the lucky one.

Somedays

Somedays…
Getting out of bed is the only battle I win.
On these days my tank runs empty
Before the day really begins.
Inner demons weigh me down
Often stealing my breath
And causing me to drown
In my own thoughts.
But a good night's rest
A glass of Rose'
We begin anew,
Tomorrow a new chance to win the battle again.

The Weight of the Mirror

I hate my body.
That's okay, it hates me too.
My inner demons are louder than thunder.
Shrieking in my ear:
>You're fat!
>You're disgusting!
>No one will ever love you at that size.
>Your own partner doesn't even want to
touch you.
>Weigh again.
>Food is the enemy
>Count the calories
>Run. Longer. Faster. Sweat it out
>Measure. Weigh. Repeat
Why won't the scale drop?
One moment I'm fine, the next filled with rage.
Filled with disgust.
Pain fills my soul. Emotional. Physical.
I cry tears in the shower, I beg my demons to
release me.
I get up tomorrow and surrender to the battle
again.

Moon Dream

What is a dream?
She asks,
But our deepest desires dancing in the pale
moonlight's shadow.

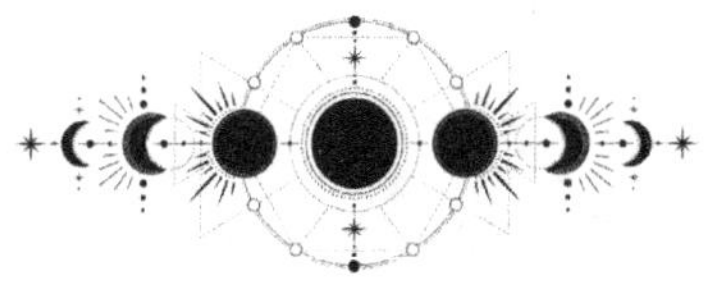

Timeless

Time, relentless, marches on
As peasants, we kneel at her throne.
In adolescence's embrace, we find,
A kaleidoscope of emotions forever intertwined
Traces of sorrow sting
Reminding me of the joy that life may bring.
Stumble. Falter. Strive.
Do something every day to feel alive.
Love fiercely, be kind hearted,
But never forget where you started.

Soul Mate's Song

Bound souls, intertwined,
Two halves united as one,
Our souls set aflame

Homecoming

In your warm embrace,
My heart finds its one true home,
My soul, set aflame.

Sacred Paradox

I look at the heavens, for whatever God will
listen,
Seeking recompense.
Looking for some defense, from my own
demons.
Begging for some revelation,
Rage ignites within every depth of my being.
The depths of my soul, a tangle of emotion.
A dance of joy. A dance of strife.
For answers, I yearn in a desperate fight.
But your mystery remains, their depths untold.

With trembling hands, I grasp the bottle
Poison flows. False power bestows.
A temporary balm is all that is found.
Slowly twisting the throttle toward
self-destruction.
Searching for God.
I call his name to no avail.
My spirit tattered.
God's illusion shattered.
I feel alone. I feel forsaken.
Faith and questions intertwine.
Doubts creep in,
Despite the scriptures I read or prayers I speak.

Somedays I feel a presence lingering, soft and wise.
A constant question, I wrestle within,
Can doubt and faith coexist?

The Puppeteer

A world of chaos and endless noise
Here I am, armed with poise.
Poise engrained in me from an early age
Sit up straight. Say, thank you. Yes ma'am. No
sir.
Don't challenge the status quo.
For years these verses I kept repressed,
Living in a world that flourished only on dreams
oppressed.

As I grow older, the bitterness unfolds,
I want to take on the world - challenge the
norms, break the mold.
A mold created from a life not my own
Go to church. Do your homework.
Make sure your chores are done. Be the good
girl to make your parents proud.
Can't anyone hear me screaming out loud
For help…

Anger festers for opportunities lost because I
was determined to please.
Anxiety eats at me, destroying me like a terrible
disease.
A disease perpetuated by patterns that confine

Questions cascade like tears, my spirit shaken
What am I to do with a life that will never be
mine?
A hurricane of words, laced with venom and
spite
Love based on fear and manipulation, with no
end in sight

I often lie awake at night listening to the clock
tick-tock-tick
Reflecting on the decisions that you made that
were purely toxic
A toxic relationship, that forced boundaries to be
created.
Painful whispers of emotion, unspoken and pure
Paint vivid scenes of passion negated.
Oft a tyrant in disguise, like a puppeteer she
pulls the strings
Dreams left shattered, only happy if others are
suffering.

I trudge forward, exploring a life on my own
Nursing the deep wounds of a venomous tongue.
A tongue that has haunted my thoughts for
years,
That fostered self - doubt in place of self-love,
That was supposed to heal me, but instead
caused many of my tears

In the depths of my mind, her voice still echoes,
pulling me back
Moving forward until I crack…
And do what she wants.

Sometimes I still surrender,
Afraid to disappoint, afraid to offend her.
But in the depths of pain, a story unfolds
With each passing day, she lessens the hold.
A hold that has crippled me for all of this time.
Shattered spirits left in her wake, picking up the
pieces,
Her hunger for control, always allowed to
dominate and define.
My every move.

This journey to liberation, a demanding fight
Turning loose of the demons and entering a
realm of light.
A realm of light that carries me away from love
gone awry.
I am courageous. I am bold.
A strength emerges the healing starts from
within
Breaking free, exiting the web, emerging numb
and cold.
A moment of silence for the wounded, and those
who've endured,

And though the pages of the past still haunt us, a
new chapter of life begins now,
in that, we can rest assured.

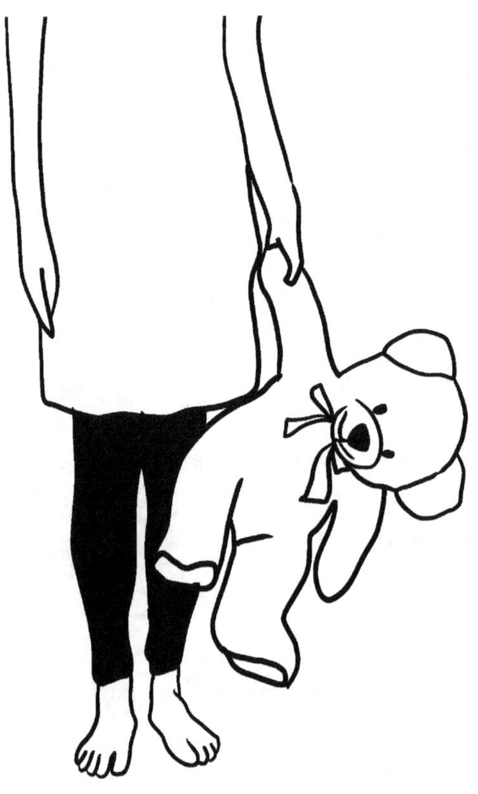

Folly Beach

Dolphins dance, waves crash and roar
A coastal gem - forevermore.
Sandy toes and salty hair.
Bliss. Serenity. Beyond compare.
Waves crash a rhythmic melody
The ocean the sincerest form of therapy.
Ocean breezes whisper secrets to the wind
The shore, a haven of hope, a place to clear the
mind.
Sunkissed bodies bask in the golden sun.
Life's simplicity and joy are truly won.
Worries fade away beneath the sun's kiss.
Embracing the serenade of the ocean's gentle
call.
Pure Bliss.

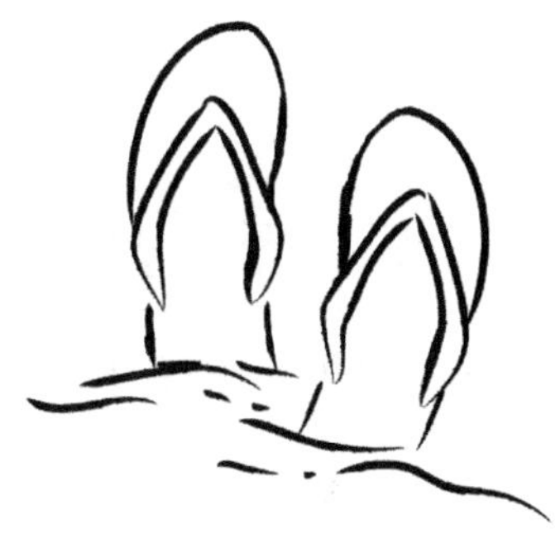

Peacefully She Sleeps

A transformation, a profound rebirth,
Peacefully she sleeps now that she knows her
worth.
In the depths of her being, a flame ignited,
A recognition of strength, long unrequited.

Once lost in the shadows of self-doubt and
despair.
A heart awakened, by basking in self-care.
Through trials and tribulations, she has
constantly roamed
Seeking the worth that had long been unknown.

No longer submitting to other's expectations,
She finds purpose, defies limitations.
She embraces her flaws, each one a testament,
To her resilience, her growth, an empowering
ascent.

She learns her worth is not tied to external
acclaim,
But rooted deep within her, is self-love that she
must sustain.
She dances to the rhythm of her own heart,
Unburdened by demons that once tore her apart.

In dreams, she glides on wings of liberation,
Breaking free from chains of wanting constant
validation.
In the silence of her peaceful sleep, her soul
rests,
A priceless gem - self-love no longer protests.

She embraces her slumber. A testament to
rebirth.
Peacefully she sleeps now that she knows her
worth.
She seeks to inspire others on their quest,
To find their own beauty within, and let their
souls
manifest.

The Funny Thing About 30

I wake up with an awful ache.
Today, there are 3 decades of candles on my
cake.
I embark on a new journey
A new decade. Vulnerable.
I am tearful.
I mourn for the nights of the decade past.
Gone are nights of reckless abandon
Sex with strangers, weekday hangovers
Fuck! That decade flew by FAST!
The last ten years, a whirlwind of exploration.
An ode to passion. To making new revelations.
Losing myself in all that it was.
Gaining scars that can't be patched up with
gauze.
The black sheep of the family is all grown up.
But I'll be damned if this isn't my best year yet.
My sites are set - go on, place your bets.
On my success. On my failure. It matters not.
With this decade I stand upon the precipice of
new adventures.
Like a butterfly, ready to emerge from her
cocoon.
A new decade of challenges
New words ignite, and flow into new passages.

As I have settled into this new phase of life
I choose not to dwell on woes of aging,
Instead I face it head on, clarity awakens,
confidence blooms.
My best days are yet to come.